FOUND VOICES

FOUND VOICES

monologues and tales

Derek Kannemeyer

Clare Songbirds
Publishing House

Clare Songbirds Publishing House Poetry Series
ISBN 978-1-957221-23-6
Clare Songbirds Publishing House
Found Voices © 2025 Derek Kannemeyer

Printed in the United States of America
FIRST EDITION

140 Cottage Street
Auburn, New York 13021
www.claresongbirdspub.com

As conceived, these pieces shared a desire to function as poetry, as short fiction, and (most of them) as spoken monologues. I'd like to dedicate the collection to my co-actors from my first ever theatrical troupe, the Artisans. And in particular to my brother Miqhey Kannemeyer, to my sister Sylvia Lamb, and to my friends Tony Winn and Sally Faraday.

ACKNOWLEDGMENTS

Thanks to the Cindy Cunningham and her co-editors at Wellspring Literary Journal, in which "Writer Unknown: A Found Journal" was first published, and to James Lewis, and his team at Verse-Virtual, who were the first publishers of "Leaving You."

I'd also like to thank the Virginia Center for the Creative Arts. It was at a residency in their Auvillar, France location that I dreamed, and mostly wrote, the tale I call "The Frame Maker's Daughter."

And most especially, a big thank you to Clare Songbirds Publishing House. Longer poems can be harder to place, and long poems which were conceived to treble as short fiction and as theatrical monologues, as most of these were, might be even more likely to fall through the cracks. Any actors who take a look at these pieces, have at them! Let me know how it goes!

CONTENTS

CONTENTS

Writer Unknown: a found journal

1. "I write journal in their language"

I write journal in their language, like teacher asks.
Not for show-me, she says, if hard to show? But write
what I observe of her country, to make sense of us.
Or write what I knew, my old life, and have lost. Share
only if I wish, for her to fix after—teach righter words.
(I understand good, but speak *half-assed*, my friend say.
Timboy. He the small boy of landlady. He is fun as shit.)

My teacher is old woman, and I am this foreigner boy,
but she lay her white warm hand softly on me: *clammy,*
she say the word is. Sorry! summer hot here! she say,
and this building bad. (*Air less,* I think say.) Oh dear,
she laughs, patting dry with cloth. She picks her hand
from my *wrist,* word I should knew, to pose on desk.
Her back of her hand sits next of my back of hand.
It have big, blue, tree root veins. Like elf writing.

There is an expression, teacher says. *To know like
the back of your hand.* Know half-assed, this mean?
This mean, see, not look good at? No, no, she laughs.
Know very well! Huh. The back of my hand all
crisscrossed (she tell word) with stitched cuts still,
from the wire, but is a young hand. Will heal. Huh,
I say. But back of hand, I ask, why even look at?
Just bony skin! But we sit. We look at the hands;
her blue veins and my scars, like there some clue
to figure, if we fit right. Maybe puzzle piece game
or assemble from kit thing or pirate treasure map.

2. I am studying after age of eight

I am studying after age of eight this language.
Am 16 now. Should know it righter, huh? But school
was not take serious always, I guess. Grammar dumb
anyway, like rules the government tells: no sense.
Vocabulary I learn more better—if you point, I go,
book, table, chair, hand, ass. Speak good is harder,
and the hearing it so fast they speak it. At food table
I fall a bit asleep, with the speaking of Mrs. Schwenk
and her Timboy, who is ten, who I understand good
if they just to *me*—but fast, *both*?—is like noise of sea.
Yeah, sure, sense bits blob through too, like wreckage
I feel the thump against, but most is noise, like surf
that crash, and batter of undertow I drown in. (Think this
in own language, and when write, ask teacher words.
She say, Oh, normal. Get harder too, sometime, like you
go digest first. Clear clogs from the head. Next day, pow,
more easy.) Meanwhile, mama so bad like me. *More* bad.
She speak with me together, though, if not too tired,
best as we can, to make better, knowing we do sound
like pair of dumbasses. Word I like. *Hey dumbass,*
Timboy teach me. *Hey, dumbass,* I say to mama,
and we giggle. (Timboy make fart noise to prove
his own ass not dumb, but I do not say to mama.)
Today Mrs. Schwenk take mama to church, to meet
the ladies. Or worship maybe? I tell Timboy of noise
of the sea, and of real sea that battering us for days,
until we sink. Luck in a million, man say who save
some of us. We clutch blob bits, not even long he say
but felt long, and we so scared still, in the man's boat,
heaving like sea. I not make clear, and Timboy polite,
but not much listen. Bits of, he pick at to pronounce
good. "Is *scared*, not scarred! *Worship*, not warship!"

3. Mama is wait in lines again, for forms

Mama is wait in lines again, for forms. That last time
I go also, interpret, but I mess up a bit too lots. Better
she make own screw-ups. No biggie, I say, government
here not scary bad people! Oh, scary a bit, she say back,
but she laugh too. There no hide good or you die bad
scary bad people. So hey, I am sit in the park right
next their offices, right in the open, on bench by water!
And I talk to ducks! (*Quack, quack,* Timboy say is what
ducks say. But not what I hear!) Now those two by edge
of lake? Kid duck and his mama? That boy duck, see,
got plastic trash catched to his leg! He make duck noise.
Mama bends low her beak, for little boy duck to pull
away from her; and plop, it tugs off of him like my sock.
She spits white filth bits after. *Plop!* go white filths also.

Lotsa ducks and goose too occupying in the carpark—
government sign say, NOT FEED THE WATERFOWL.
You too many, I tell goose who swims the bank at me,
nibbling up the plants. *Humans can't feed all!* But I guess
he got to ask anyway. Waddle waddle honk! *Not got food,
sorry. You guys too many!* But summer, green things grow,
and our earth provides. With sun, it grow fat and lovely.
So he got grasses! For me, got apple and soda! No one die!
Know what? I tell goose. *I dispose this here bad people
trash for you. In proper receptacle, out of waterfowl harm.*

4. I am not writing in journal for a while

I am not writing in journal for a while. Things are
not worst, but not greatest. Mama, who is a hospital
nurse in our country, must study to do that kinda
work here. And must talk better also. It will happen,
they say, they will put in classes, so she will learn.
Mama cries, but is not so bad-bad. She has a job
of shops cleaning for now. The bus takes long,
but they say "honest work." Know what? Me too!
I sell, door to door for Mrs. Schwenk, orders for
cakes she bakes! Just till summer over, and teacher
fix me up for school. There is a nice dog today
I make friends with at a house I ring their bell for.
Most house nobody there, or not come see, or they
not think me "honest work," but some, so feel safe,
bring doggy. And this pooch jump up to love me.
Tail, I say, as she go hoppy wag. *Ear,* and I scratch
her ear. I know good my body parts vocab for maybe
most parts now, I tell the lady, who smiling. Her Bitsy
rubs against me. And I rub Bitsy gentle on *belly* and on
what of the neck I learn is called the *scruff.* (*You can't
go out all scruffy,* told Mrs. Schwenk. She fixes me
good clothes, trims the hair of my neck, the *scruff.*)
The hair flat by Bitsy's collar is thick and ginger,
and she likes when I press my hand to scrub where
she itchy. Where the collar and scruff *chafe*—this
lady teach word. And score! Lady buy my cake!

5. This country, it got all kind of sports

This country, it got all kind of sports. Sports
which you throw, you catch, you run. Nets sports!
Sports where there big hits with sticks! You gotta
know sports, dude! Timboy shout to me. You wanna
fit in here? This sport, that sport, you learn *lotsa*
sports. And you got a lil money now, right, dude?
Okay, got some. (Not lot, but I know to say, *Okay,*
and act like.) So you need your own glove now,
right? he asks. I can get you one in not so rough
shape, maybe five bucks, max. So I say, *Cool,*
and soon I got me a glove, not new but not rough,
and Timboy and me, we throwin'. The ball a more
wildfly bird than balls back where I come from—
it coiled tighter, I guess—so it has lift-off at you—
why sometimes I hang my glove too low—and this
one time it gobsmacks me in the chin. Like, pow!
But worse is when Timboy throws it a bit big
and me with my glove wrong, and the dumbass
ball bust the shed window. Dude, cries out Timboy,
can't you catch a lick? Well, I guess not, lil buddy.
The shed is locked, but we peep through the hole
where the ball go and I spy it. Some flower pots
and puddle of maybe not so cheap glass around it.
Squish my face to the wood frame to look in good,
and ow, knock the sore spot, where it now hatching,
like new egg at my lip, where I take it on the chin.

5

6. I like this room, the sunroom

I like this room, the sunroom. Will miss.
This red round lacquer table. White blinds
like skimpy ladders, for light of sun
to sneak through rungs. Mrs. Schwenk says,
"Study in here today, dear—I will help you."
Her house is too small for us "long term,"
she decide last night, after the man fix window.
But she'll give two weeks to look. "So sorry!"

This morning, to be more nice, she walks mama to the bus.
She smiles to me. She sets pot of scented tea on the red table.
No news about your dad? she asks. No, ma'am, still missing.
Timmy misses his dad too, she says, like let that explain us.
(Timboy and me in *doghouse*, Timboy tell me.
"Our yard not for ball-throwing, and you know that, mister!")

Vocab list 27 is where I am reached today.
Stamina. Insomnia. Agenda.
Mrs. Schwenk says definitions from the flashcards,
my words ending in letter *A*, until I know them.
Aroma, for which I smell the tea, say *Ah!* We laugh.
Chutzpa, I speak wrong. Okay, say Mrs. S., but speak right!
You gonna need some of that there *chutzpa* in this country!
Dilemma. Most we spell it *chutzpah*, though, she tells me,
a-h, still on the old word. The blinds' lines of shine
and shadow let the dark and light in. Some bars of them
on Mrs. Schwenk, some bars behind her, less wavier,
on the wall. Not all the way whites and blacks like book print,
though—more soft, like skins; colors of my skin, her skin.
Except same shine-shadow skin, like stripes of *zebra*.

7. There is a aid organization

There is a aid organization—*The Friends,* it means,
but it has the *friends* word in our language. Friends people,
long time, arrive here from our country. But lotsa aid groups!
Like *Refugee Resettlement* is government, like *New Roots,*
which is church, like the language tutors at the *R.L.C.*
Lotsa folks who mean good here. So what if the gov org
is scary a bit, and gee louise their forms? So what if maybe
New Roots have an "agenda"? Be as it may, *Friends*
is who fix us up with Mrs. Schwenk. *Friends* is how
we been in this house. So *Friends* is mama say to call.

Uh-oh, I think to me. I don't like the *Friends* folks much.
The old ones do not know or understand, since they long gone,
but they are so sure they do. The youngs have skimpy sense of
but at least don't care. Young *Friend* fetched us at the airport,
down big, big roads sun-splintered with big, bright cars—
not speaking us in our language (because not know well),
but singing a song we learned as little: a song of revolution,
that she not seem to know say, kill our people. "Sing with,
sing with!" *Sorry, don't sing too good,* mama telling her.
She put a window down and I hanged my head out like a dog.
See green fields, forests, rivers. Choke a bit on stink of fuel.
This Friend woman say, "This is called the Bible Belt."
And then while she singing more, real loud, with the radio,
a police wail pull us stopped. We are speeding. His name
says *OFFICER BIBLE.* "Oh fuck!" the Friend woman saying,
real soft, when she sees his name. Legit, that was his name,
Officer Bible! So Friend woman very polite to Officer Bible.
His face, it shows her nothing—it's not a mean look;
more so a hard look, like he one of the tanks of the military.
Our Friend hands him her forms. Mama asks, he want ours?
But only the Friend's forms needed. Slowly, so slowly,
this policeman looks, then looks again at them. Like he thinking,
Lady, are you friend or foe? Court date July 27. That when
they decide, maybe, which one is she, if she belong here yet.

8. This new place we got

This place we got, not so far! *Keep same school zone,*
everyone say, so mama be ridin' that same ol' bus ride still.
But she'll find a more close job, hopefully. Timboy say
he'll cycle to visit us, dude, which Mrs. Schwenk
don't seem so happy at. (*He not your brother,*
he says she tell him, *and you too little for his friend.*)
Timboy, I say, forget me, dude, I'm trouble for you.
But our last days—last before school also—
we go camp out in the sunroom, at that ol' red table,
and he teachin' me card games. Crazy eights, one called.
Bit fun, bit boring. Know poker, Timboy? I ask. I teach!

Was at internment camp I learned. We played for rocks.
Dirt floors, some fat shade trees. Was okay there, I reckon.
Not safe always, if you think you more smart, but okay,
as long as you not poke your head. You can wait the time.
Even with poker. Mama said, *Keep the head low. Don't
anger the hard men to win big! We just want get our forms.*
Oh, I listened. It just good sense. I had a lizard short time,
pet for a day, it *think* it smart? It poke its head.
Then pow, quick, gobbled, like a wink!

Timboy not bad. Don't hide his cards good, holds low
when he check his phone, but he do have chutzpa.
Gonna find some chumps, when his school start back,
he say, and not for no *play* stakes, neither. *Real* money.
Get *rich* a little. Uh-oh, you trouble like me, Timboy!
We the trouble brothers, dude, he say. Nah, I tell him,
that not smart. Keep the head low. Let the little
green lizards make the dumbass move, get eat.

9. We on the fifth floor here

We on the fifth floor here. A new new place, east side,
coz first new place "fell through." I nervous to ask!
But just mean we didn't get. So this one. Walls thin,
neighbors loud, funny smells. Little ugly, but it's *ours*,
mama says. She is worried, coz I'm not sleeping right.
Three nights the weather bad, all kaboom of thunder.
We got no curtains, so weird shapes let into the room
when a lightning smacks it. It a bit like this movie I saw,
I say to my Learning Center tutor—*boom! flash bomb!*—
then when the flickers go dark again your eyes got wild
bad pictures. When for the real of it it's just my pants
slung over the chair lumpy, or my shirt swinging a bit
where I hung it. Not some dead thing all flung up there.
She asks many questions over this. Just to care, be nice.
Like some she asks because the Friends have got me
into this different school now, this religious school?
RLC teacher she say, uh-oh, she don't know about that.

She worries too much, though, like mama. Like maybe
I sleep bad coz my dumbass life has been so scary.
Nah, I say, it's just loud here, and the cot too hard.
Uh-huh, she says. Ma'am, I say, the thunder
is nothing like no bombs, if that's your worry.
With thunder there's a sweetness in the air, you know?
The way the rain raise up the, the… Fragrances,
she say. The fragrances. And I am snug in my sheet
on the floor, mostly, lately, coz the cot also too narrow,
and on the cot now I got my school books spread out,
so if the bad men come with bayonets, all they'll get
to stab will be my algebra! Nah, ma'am, I'm good.

10. You faking with me, boy?

You faking with me, boy? says the Counselor. *Like
I don't know you learning English since you eight?*
Look, I want to tell her. At eight, one day a week,
I *start* school. I taught to *count*. At ten I go more,
but the rains bad, the river big, school close for months.
When twelve, I needed for *work* work. For kids like me,
I want to say, I speak good! So I angry, but she is true:
ten weeks here—and I still feel like I am a dumbass.
I do! Which should on no account spill *guts* of! But she
keep not seeing me, see label this, label that—I got
who *you* are, mister. So I poke head, for *real*, to *tell*!
Which is dumbass. Coz her eyes all, *Oho, I thought so.*
But I still saying! And saying it *more* wrong! I for real
cry, wow, like the rains that close the school! This lady,
she a bit nice at that, coz I so pitiful. Also coz *gotcha.*
Lays hand on top my back of, like friends. Bit more
to trap it. She holds her papers made for the nose at me.
She waits I stop. Then quiet, she say, *Listen. Listen.*
I gotta be put back, just for now, with the littler kids.

The school here tough. The teachers don't put up,
way they say it, with no darn hooey. You talk back—
you look at shit during prayer time—just you list
new word in journal—they *take* your shit. They *confiscate.*
(Fancy word for take!) Gimme that, what is this *hooey*?
How the heck help you to write, write all wrong English?
Dispose in receptacle! Copy out is better a few prayers!

Fine, put me back with the littler kids. But lady,
why you *like* when you think me weak? Like I'm
the crybaby boy, the shows you his cards boy,
like I can't read what deal I got? Counselor, I did
terrible things, once. I am not your dumbass pet
gets eat. You do not know how hard a boy I been.

So we sit, her palm on top my back of. Real gently,
eyes down, no chutzpa, I press my other hand. I find
for her a face. Not angry face. Not a bit quiet angry.
Only the needing nice boy, the bit scared good boy.
Smiling like shy, like trying not to cry no more.
Thank you, Dr. Solomon. Help me be better.

The Last Time I Played Truth or Dare

1.
"Steal something," Billy said. "From the Prince's Minimart.
And Jill, not an inkpen either, something with some heft to it."
His spread fingers around my nipple gently tightening. *Asshole,*
I thought, but would not say, would not give him the pleasure.
Old Mr. Prince had gone from courtly to creepy as he aged;
the rare times I still went there I could feel his eyes crawling
me as I shopped—Billy knew this. "I can't do this," I murmured.
"Fine. So Truth, then?" Billy asked. I was 23, 24, living with
a sweet, dumb bully who thought I'd marry him, "I can't do this"
was the truth. "It was you picked Dare," he said to my silence.
It was early evening, late September, both the windows cracked,
waft of the curtains and the sheets untucked, him spooning with
his arm hooked under mine, across my breast. Often after sex,
less often lately, one of us said, "Truth or Dare," and always
we said, "Truth." And then we'd whisper things; it was nice.
But tonight, knowing what he'd have asked, about whom he'd ask,
I'd chosen Dare…
        At work the next day, David and I
broke up. If you can call it breaking up when you've never
done more than flirt, and wished you had the guts, or when
you're not done wishing it. "Whatever this is we're doing,"
I said, "we've got to stop." And after a moment he said, "Yes."

2.
So that night, well after midnight, no one around, I drove
to the Prince's Minimart with a folding ladder, to struggle it
from the trunk and pry the big white wooden apostrophe
from the storefront's sign. I was slighter of frame then,
and everything about that night felt way too big for me:
the ladder, the fat country sky of stars, the full moon hanging
low and watching. Not least this thing going wrong in me—
like a break-up with myself, or a fire between the world
and me I couldn't fight through any more. You know
those two or three moments, from all the years you've
been alive, you can think back and you're still right there?
This night's that way. My insides roiling, and the rattle
of metal rungs dragged up the curb, and the sweat collecting
at my tee-shirt's neck. And then as I teetered the ladder
upright, the panic that it was slipping, was about to smash
through the storefront's glass. But somewhere a street or two

over I heard a car, and froze on a step, and it calmed me.
It's a prank, I thought, *what's the worst they could do to me?*
If Billy weren't such an ass, I thought, *if I weren't so pissed*
at him, I might even find this funny. Or fun. Or you know,
beautiful, the sweet night air, the stars... And then that brawl
I'd been having with my life? It let up suddenly like a weight—
such useless ugliness. Or like a snarl traced back to work
it clear—the seeing how to work it clear, and that it *would*;
that *this*, right *now*, would free me...
                      So I climbed, I
paused on the top rung, just right, and I braced with the flat
of a hand against the E. The apostrophe came free so easily
it startled me: two tugs with a lever, and it unstuck, and it
pinwheeled up. On impulse—whether from glee of mischief
or because the grammar I was making bugged me—I worked
the two screws loose that held the S and took that too.

3.
I've never *not* thought about that night really—how could
I forget, what with the Prince Minimart still in operation
and his grandkids not bothering to fix the sign—but it's
been more so recently, because David and I have sons
now at the same school as Billy and his wife, and there
was a reception last week that they hosted.
                            "Hey, Jill,"
Billy said, "let me show you something—down here..."
We were in his basement workshop; he'd flicked a light;
there were letters of mismatched styles and sizes, screwed
in a wall over the workbench, spelling *Bill's Trophy Room.*
As we stood and looked. Me at the S and the apostrophe
and him at me. "I bought the rest," he said. "Less obvious."
I nodded, flummoxed, and he followed me back up.

4.
So a few nights later, my hand crooking his shoulder's
curve, I say to David, "Truth or Dare." Not real loud, not
waking him; just so I can think if the story means much—
the way it once meant. There was once an apostrophe,
also an S, which I stole and gave to Billy, so I could
take back myself...
               Well, good luck to him. That's
all the truth of it. *Dare, then*... And as sleep comes,
I'm away again climbing that high ladder, into this breath
of almost fall weather air. This unstuck self. These stars.

Daddy Shows and Tells

So. You're my daughter's classmates! It's very nice
to be with you today. And Cindy, so this is your classroom,
well isn't it lovely! And you have a turtle! I had a turtle,
I was about your age, in fact. Little Gerry! I'm not sure
what became of Gerry. He wasn't an *active* pet, I think I
may have lost interest in him. Anyway. My collection.
Because I hear you're having the *dads* in, checking us out,
right? And we're to talk about whatever it is we *collect*,
is that right? Well let's hope so, because that's what
I've brought! I doubt even my daughter's seen this box,
have you, sweetie? No? Know what daddy's got in his
box of treasures? Any of you other girls want to guess?
No? Then let's see, shall we, if I can just... Grab a fistful...
There. You know the names of any of these, girls?
That's right, a kazoo! And a rattle! And in fact
I don't know what you'd *call* this one, something that
goes clack clack when you go like this, anyway, *clack*
clack clack clack. Clack clack! You like that? So these
are my noisemakers, because what I collect are noisemakers,
and here they are, my noisemakers! No, dear, that's a
nose-flute, you may not want it in your mouth, they don't
actually share well. No by all means take a *look*, dear,
let your *hand* look, I mean, but perhaps put the others
back in the baggie? There. Much better. In fact I have
four boxes, this one and three more I've got all
neatly catalogued, but the others are like the *good* china,
plus a lot to lug, so I thought just the *cheap* noise today!
My hodgepodge box, I call it. Here, go on, dip a paw in,
pluck out a plum, try out your sound... Come on now,
huff, puff, thump, thwack, shake, rattle, roll, don't be shy!
Yay, that's it, good, yes, not bad for a first go! I can't wait
to hear the second go! We'll try a second go shortly!
But hush a moment, hush now, I think I'm supposed
to talk first, right—do the tell as well as the show?
Say why noisemakers? Well, it began in college,
before Cindy was born or I met her mother. I was in a band.
Well, *with* the band, to be honest, a roadie and a toady,
I didn't sing or *play*, but then it wasn't really that kind
of band. Or it was, but not only. We were a *show*!
Dancers, lights, fake blood, smells, smoke and spectacle!
I was what we called the Noiseman. I brought the Noise.
We had this one song, our signature song,

where noise was the chorus. I'd come on between songs—
after the song before—and the drummer would lay down
this chugga-chig-*cheee*, and he'd say, "And now, Neil the
*Noiiise*man!"—and I'd teach the audience how to make noise
with all my noisemakers in turn, and I'd pass them around
till the hall was wall to wall ca*cop*h*ony—at which point
I would go, "Heeere comes the Noise!", and the band would
just raunch-launch into "Here Comes the Noise", of which
the chorus was the singer screeching, "Here comes the noise!"
while the band and the crowd went nutso loud!
So, I was Neil the Noiseman! I was Neil the Noiseman
for about eight months, in fact, but then the band
kind of changed, and I kind of met Cindy's mom,
and she thought the Noise was kind of infantile,
to tell the truth. I told her that was kind of the *point*,
but I guess that's what girls do, isn't it, girls, tell the boys
when it's time to grow up and stop being infantile?
They wait till they have us at their mercy, if that's
a way to explain it a little in present company,
and they say, "Neil, it's kind of infantile. It's time
to grow up, and if you like I'll help you," and I
kind of said, "That's kind of you." So, anyway:
I didn't bring *all* the noise today—also, look, ma, no band—
but maybe there's enough in the old hodgepodge box
for a little *gurrl* noise, if maybe you girls are
brat enough to have some real kid noise in you?
What do you think, do you think so? Don't go telling,
but I think I still am! I mean it's not like I *mind*
the quiet, but sometimes I need a *change*, you know?
I mean sometimes living with Julie and Cindy it gets
so quiet I want, well, quite honestly I want to scream,
you know? Just sometimes? Oh dear, Cindy's all
embarrassed now, don't look at Cindy, girls,
her mother's embarrassment gene has kicked in;
but secretly she's a bit like her ol' dad too—
I bet if you give me one good *scream* when I say,
"Here comes the scream!" we'll get her screaming with.
Then in a minute we'll make our noisemaker noise—
I mean, *really* make it, after we *scream*, once the scream
gets us started—like a starter's pistol! So, noisemakers
ready, girls, I'll count us in—noisemakers, good—one,
two, two and a half, three: here comes the *screaaaam!*

Leaving You

"I promise to take you everywhere, my lovely child,
and then to leave you."

~Max Apple, "Bridgings"

We glimpse the stone hump of the bridge, and you
clamber across the footpath's turns, through rocks
and scrub brush, to peer from the overlook
and spy the river. *Be careful,* I call,
making my slower way—though more to hail
you than in warning; we trust each other,
we two; and you wave, hallooing back. When
I reach you, you're rested, and I might wish
I were less short-breathed. But yes, one hill left,
since look, that glint's the river, and across
the bridge the city, and this bench, to sit
flank to shoulder, in pledge of steadiness.

How long have we been walking now, sweetheart,
I ask, *is it twelve years? Sixteen, daddy,*
you say, knowing I'm teasing and must know.
Oddly, though, I've begun to forget things.
When we set out, wasn't someone with us,
your mom, I must mean? And didn't I come
this way once with my parents? *Remember,
darling,* I ask instead, *how I'd carry
you sometimes?* You laugh. *And there was a dog,*
you say. *Trixie!* I say back. *You'd lurch off
after her. I had to catch hold of you,
till you learned that where we led, she'd follow.*

We're walking again, in step, side by side.
We'll get there by my half-birthday, bet you,
you say, without impatience: the way down
is sunlit, our stride a strong, shared heartbeat…
But then as the bridge draws closer, your pace
starts to flag. On the other side there are
so many roads, and you know without talk
of it that I will be done with leading—
that we won't always favor the same ones;
which is fine, except for the maze they'll be,

and this fear you can't say, that our windings
may not much meet. *Oh, it'll be fine, love,*
I tell you without words—with smiles; a hand
reached wide behind me. *I know this journey;
I've come this way, and there is no other.*
Still, for a bit, what say we don't cross yet?
We'll look only, and count all the coppery
swift colors in the slapping water—
and loll upslope to share our sandwiches—
puttering by the bend where the wildflowers
flutter—to twine our two sprigs of them. Then,
when it's time, I'll nod back once and go; not
stopping, or slowed to see; till behind me
I'll hear the sturdy engine of your breath.

On the Island of Wild Dogs

1.
Come with, he said. You believe in this world
no more than I do, do you deny it?
I do not deny it, she said. But Peter,
I am very young. *We* are very young.
He laughed. Just young enough! No, quickly now,
Caitlin, while we still dare... Across the waves
nothing of the island was visible,
but he had sailed to it; he knew where it lay.
He took her by the shoulders and turned her,
gently, firmly, to face his promise of it.
There in the clifftop's sedge they stood awhile,
alone under the sky. A spring wind gusting.
About them, the cawing and capering gulls.
So they married, and she went. Oh, why not,
after all: Peter loved her. Or at least
found her beautiful—so thought he loved her;
which might suffice. She needed to be loved,
or wanted. The crossing churned her stomach,
but this sea where she had loosed her father's
ashes would not harm her; she was not scared.
Her mother, still grief-ridden, still anchored
to her rooms, went small behind her much as
the world did: for a while invisible;
then perhaps only imaginary.

The lighthouse cottage—but he'd told her this—
was robustly charmless. Five compact rooms;
stone walls sturdy enough to shelter them.
The lantern room, by contrast, set atop
its tower—a verdigris spiral staircase,
up to a rose-slabbed glass nook—was lovely,
although barred to her. A man-cave, had she
known the term, good only for one; for him.
A desk: his desk; a cot, where he stretched out,
reading, sleeping. As was required, sometimes;
as was his duty. She was unsure why.
There was little shipping. Though there were storms,
and fogs, and to keep the light was his charge.
She bowed to that. Besides, when he had time,
he smiled and was kind. She was, she assured
herself, content. Besides, she had her dogs.

2.
For theirs was an island of dogs: the dogs
were why the posting called for a couple.
The oversight of the dogs was her charge.
A frivolous cause, of course, the welfare
of stray mutts, yet it charmed her. The recluse
whose estate this island once was, whose will
provided for them, had termed the ownership
of dogs, unless in working partnership—
bird dogs, hunters, service dogs—"a scandal";
to keep pets "a simpering enslavement."
For the love of all things wild, he'd bequeathed
to the dogs his land, to breed, and swarm it,
sovereign and free. So they came—and thrived,
though every provision ship brought more.
There was acreage, on the heaths, in the caves;
there was game enough: the gophers, the rabbits
Caitlin laid in her carrots for; there was
her stewardship to smooth the way. Hers were
the crops and the paths. Hers were the paddocks,
where the new dogs came to acculturate,
great fenced-in places where they might form packs;
not fall prey to the packs already formed...

3.
"Consider," my father broke in (whose tale
this was, told by the den fire, one winter
when I came needing its comfort), "how hard
your great-grandmother must have found it all,
Mikey. Not because she loved animals
too much, or little; the executors
did ask. *Fond enough to mind one,* she'd said.
No wish to call one mine. Such gangs of such
wild dogs, though? And the isolation! No
phones, back then. Just one boat, monthly... Of course,
you might see the lure. Caitlin was *like* you,"
my father said—not unkindly; merely
as if something for me to think about—
"by her nature solitary; her husband
should be company enough. She'd *thought* that."

4.
And he might be. In good time. Yes, they fought.
But not with fists, or hard words. A silence
would turn angry. There was a sullenness
in her she had not known of until he
wakened it. A bullheaded deafness in him
she had not supposed. He *pronounced*, sometimes.
Then withdrew, clank of boots, clicked lock, upstairs.
She wrapped herself against the cold and walked,
into the rain, the mist, a storm. Most times
not heedlessly: she stayed to the main paths,
and she took a gun. The dogs sought neither
to beseech nor bully her, but there were
lines, Peter said, one must draw with such beasts.
Her shotgun, shouldered, sketched hers in the air.
A squiggle... The evening of the storm, though,
she'd been in some distress; had fled, and come
back to herself, unarmed, out by the caves.
And when the lightning swarmed near, she had risked—
soaked through, shivering, far from help—their shelter.
Into the cave mouth she chose, some light reached;
back of her, down its blacker throat, seeped none.
But a snuffling rose from it, more of
distress than warning, which she turned to face.
Her eyes adapted: a mother; a new pup.
Two shapes; four eyes, a low, small shift of coals.
Neither animal, she guessed, quite healthy.
But they watched her watch, for ten long minutes;
the held stillness of a truce; until she
bobbed her head, *God bless,* and turned, and tore off
homeward through the drenching dark... By daylight,
a half day later, bearing food, she found
only the smell of them, musty and sour.
If they were to die, they would die elsewhere,
it would seem, where no human left her smell.

5.
There were some dogs who had never been strays.
Pets: once cosseted, now orphaned, or with
or without regret cast off; unhumaned.
She found herself drawn to study those ones,
though without favoritism—resolved
not to coddle as *she* might want coddling—
only attuned to the wound left by loved

then loved no longer—trusting it would heal.
She liked that it did heal, usually.
But the step proved small from there to a more
active interest; to just whom she might save.
She tried to discuss it with Peter, once.
The words, though, failed her. He rolled into sleep,
away. *Your* business, Caitlin, he mumbled...
Her business; hers alone... She may have smiled.

6.
She had been warned not to accept the dogs
too small, too fat, too old, but sometimes did.
(Even too big was a risk. One huge hound
declined to join a pack; two rival packs,
as she watched, allied to rip it apart.)
She was careful, knowing what could happen:
but *her business*, yes? Let her gauge those risks.
So sometimes some pooch would catch her fancy,
and she'd let it uncrate; shepherd it through.

One dog, though—just once—she made a pet of.
The day she knew she was pregnant again
(there had been a wisp of an earlier child,
miscarried), or feared, or hoped she must be,
there came a shipment, and it was this dog
she told it to: a terrier, too old,
too small, still pet-collared; too tame, with a
name tag she bent to read that called him SOOT.
Not fat, though; well-toned, solid. *Soot,* she said,
I think I'm pregnant, and he licked her face.

7.
We paused then. My mother brought us biscuits,
two cups of tea. It was January,
and snowing. I had spent Christmas alone.
But when they called, *Come home,* I made the trek.
And my father told and told his tales... "Well,
which is it now?" mom asked. "Surprisingly,"
I said, "not one I've heard." Dad gave a smile,
private and unreadable. Mom snorted.
She cleared his empty shot glass. I picked up
the chart of his mother's family tree
that we'd side-trailed from into anecdote.

("Here. It's just the names left, now, though, Mikey.
The stories were all on your pop pop's side.
Lord, how that man could talk!") As I fingered
the knotty squiggle of the lives branching
up and round her. May Beaufort, dad's mom's name;
Vera Watts, his mother's mother's... "That child,
though, Mikey? Your great-uncle? What a birth."
"Oh?" I said, and put down the chart to hear.

8.
But first (dad said) that dog. Ma Caitlin's good
luck charm; the dog, called by his secret name,
she held back in the pens for all her months
of pregnancy. *Soot,* she whispered to him,
and so *Soot* he stayed; as dogs came and shed
their names all round him, and poured out into
the island heaths and high lands in their packs.
Perhaps they smelled the difference of him,
and so forged no bond with him; perhaps some
tinge of deference, to this elder dog
who had welcomed them, and lodged there with them,
clung a while when they left him for the wilds.
Or threads of both. Soot had Caitlin's favor—
discreetly, since Peter must not suspect;
Soot had her trust, to help assimilate
the newcomers: more working dog than pet.
He learned his place, as the dogs all learned it,
as only Caitlin failed to: for her, Soot
was who her heart leaned on, needed, might not
bear the strain of those months without. *Peter,*
she might whisper at night, and he would be
tender with her, for a while, placate her,
with words and with touch, and sometimes even
he might listen; but placating was what
it was. When she said *Soot,* though? Soot was hers.

9.
Then the midwife came. To give birth safely—
or *more* safely, anyway—as I warned
before I would likely tell you, Caitlin—
you'll need to leave the island. But the dogs?
The dogs? What of them? The dogs will manage.
Just accept no more, for now. Clear the pens.

Leave the island for Peter to govern.
But— But *what*, Caitlin? Leave your foolishness.
In two months, when I come back, you sail with.
For the mainland. Tell your husband. *Today*,
Caitlin. Let him help with the arrangements…
So that night she told him. And he listened,
was tender with her: yes, and yes. Of course,
my love, yes, Caitlin. Until—not that night—
six weeks after that night—she told him, *Soot*.

They fought, of course. No, Caitlin, I will not
care for it. No, Caitlin, you may not take
it with you. Caitlin, you have your duty,
as I have mine. Which we will do. The packs
will tear him to bits, Peter. Will they, though?
Some may recall the dog fondly… And so—
not that day, for though angry, her husband
was a considerate man; but before
the supply boat came for her—Peter bore
this Soot in a sack to the far reaches
of the island, where he fed and left it.
Leashed with a frayed rope he hoped wouldn't be
too hard to struggle free of. Good luck, Soot,
he said, with a frown. His duty, of course,
but a hard duty. And came back to stand
over Caitlin in her bed, her small hands
outspread on her great belly, her shoulders
shrunk from him, and told her: My love, it's done.

10.
"Unhappy marriages are all alike,"
my mother instructed me, "whatever
Tolstoy may allege." *Unhappy*, she claimed,
was where one mate or both had given way.
Were there happy ones? Perhaps her parents'
had been. Who but they could know? Most of us,
Michael, muddle through. One tries, as one must,
to manage one's balance of two people
and share strain; to bear pain as best one may.
"Mom, did you love daddy?" I had asked her.
This was after he died. "Well, I miss him,
you know," she said. "Great pigheaded old goat."

23

11.
So Caitlin—if *her* marriage was to die,
it would not be that she gave way and let
it die—rose in the night from bed, after
two days of tossing in her fret and rage,
and dressed. She found her rifle and her lamp.
She would find her dog. She slipped from the house,
into the dark of their island of dogs,
and walked, or waddled, under its wild stars,
to stand her wild ground and turn; to face where
her husband slept, and come back to him whole.

12.
Well, such was the plan. Her body willed things
otherwise. The child willed things otherwise:
contractions that banged at her spine like fists.
There was a cave she'd taken shelter in—
was it eighteen months ago? She reached it.
She sprawled there. Oil light made shine and shadow
of the rock wall it ledged to ten yards back,
where once she'd watched a bitch succor her pup.
She struggled to its cleft, to fit herself
as best she could where a roof and shale walls
might enclasp her. She lay panting, gasping.
Outside, a howl of dogs she had been half
aware of for some time now grew louder,
closer, more multiple: call and answer.
Were they gathering to the lamp she had
set down? Perhaps to the blood smell of her?
She did not know. She could not, having her
own more pressing matters to attend to,
sift the thought. But she raised up a little
and aimed the gun, wavering, at the cave's
lamp-bleary mouth. Then fell—so my father's
father's mother's tale goes—in pain, distress,
in exhausted befuddlement, asleep.

13.
I know nothing of birth. I was not at
my daughter's birth, nor held her after it,
nor held her mother after it, nor did
we talk of it. Nor spoke too much at all,
since who was I, now, to talk to? Or hold,

24

ever again? We'd let those tensions fail.

But there was a woman, once, I came from,
whose birth story was told me at third hand—
or fourth, or fifth, who knows—who, so it's said,
dozed, in some fitful fashion, in a cave;
to wake to the snap, snarl of dogs at it,
fighting; who saw a dog she loved shove through
a smoke blear of lantern-flame and half-dream,
ripped-eared and bleeding; to stand guard by her—
to snarl, snap, as other dogs pursued him;
dogs she fired on, yowling, until they fled.
Till in pain *she* yowled, as Soot stood sentry.
Who stood guard through the hours she took to crouch,
and rise, and arch, and push, and defecate;
to lurch, pushing, to her knees and elbows;
while the lamp burned low, and darkness ate it;
until she lay with her child beside her;
until her dog barked her husband's hail in;
to this impregnable triad of them—
as a daylight pale as breath brimmed round them.

14.
It was my father, whom I loved dearly,
but knew as one knows a father, less as
a whole man than the player of his parts,
who told me this: this family story.
Most family stories are five parts myth
to one part true—or fair—I've tried to tell
my daughter. Our memories, as they make
their shaggy dog way to a present point,
have their axe to grind it; to some harsher
or prettier sharpness they prefer… Yet
we tell them anyway. They're what we have.
What got us here. Who hurt, failed, loved us here.

This tale, I heard years back, the year dad died.
What more of it there was, he couldn't say.
"Scrags of other folk's lives are all you get,
Mikey. Go mend *your* life. Let the wild dogs
of theirs run free." At dad's wake, my sister
said he'd told her it once too: a tamer
version, when she was small, wanting a dog.
(To placate her, since good, brave Soot was all

the dog she got.) Claiming Caitlin herself
had told him it—about *her* father's birth—
or grandfather's—who knew, now? "But a boy
was born to us," dad said. "A good, brave boy."

Elsa Walks the Plank

There was a Goss girl ten years older than Lucy, called Elsa; I met her at their family beach house, the summer before I turned 19.

As a kid sister, Lucy surprised me—she was animated, doting. We hung out at their pool and she tugged on Elsa's arm and said, *Elsa, show Ricky how to walk the plank!* Without warning, all Lucy's studied and invulnerable cool had morphed into a sack of giggles, to be shaken out and spilled in tribute at her sister's feet.

Their parents used to keep a boat, Lucy explained, and to walk the plank, how she and Elsa walked the plank, you got someone to bind your hands behind you with a scarf and force you off the side. If you were like Elsa, you knifed in so beautifully the splash was sucked in after you, like in the Olympics, and you just *kept* sinking until you were invisible, until the bad guys were sure you must have hit bottom and drowned.

Whereas in *fact* you were only waiting to clear the hull so you could kick your way under it, and resurface on the other side and pull yourself up on deck, wearing the scarf around your head bandanna-style and cackling like a pirate.

Elsa smiled mysteriously but didn't deign to respond in words. Her swimsuit was a black one-piece of the same opacity as her sunglasses, and about all I recall her doing that week was to lie back in the beach chair and let the sun have at her.

Couldn't you show me? I asked Lucy.

Not like Elsa, she said. I was little then. But I did figure out the scarf. You kind of stretch and somersault through it in the water bringing your arms round in front of you.

Loudly, Elsa yawned. It was deliberate, of course, to silence us and require our attention, and when we looked, she spoke. Her voice was low and lazy, as if she were tired, half-asleep, or bored, but I couldn't not listen to it; for one thing, she'd said almost nothing my entire visit, and so I was curious; but mostly it was her tone. Lucy and I were kids, faking having something sharp and true to say, but only blathering; Elsa, the whisper of my teen angst told me, was faking the casualness and the dispassion.

27

She said: Walking the plank is a Hollywood invention. What they did was keelhaul you. They'd tie you to a rope that ran under the boat and they'd drag you from one side to the other so that you smashed against the hull. And sorry, but you didn't get to sneak up on them afterwards. They'd <u>pull</u> you up; admire the damage. And then if you'd really pissed them off, and were still just a tiny bit alive, they would pitch you back in again.

Jeez, I said.

As you say, said Elsa, and resumed her sultry immobility.

There was a short, reflective silence. Lucy broke it as soon as she decently could. *Elsa had this boyfriend,* she giggled. *Once when she was supposed to be babysitting me, she got him to come to the boat and she walked the plank for him naked.*

Late that evening, when Lucy and I were the only ones at the house, we rummaged through the closets and found two long silk scarves, one for each of us. We slipped into the pool and she tied my hands in front of me, and I tied hers behind. She somersaulted around in the water a few times until her body remembered the trick of things, and she could pull the scarf and her bound arms out before her. Then she did it again in reverse.

What I don't get is how she keeps her breath, she said, splashing and frowning, working her bound arms back in front. I stood in the shallow water, content to watch, my arms bent before me as if in prayer, my hands still tied. *So how did your sister get those scars?* I asked.

Lucy snorted. (There were no scars on Elsa, no marks visible at all.) *Fraidycat,* she said, splashing around and around, going under and coming up again, her arms hiding their secret behind her back, her arms out in front again to show me, her arms gone back behind.

Wow, look at the stars! I said.

There they were suddenly, so many of them, silver and shimmering in the clear, dark sky.

Vineyard

I'm in the vineyard when the neighbor's boy,
tendril to any trellis, tropes by to talk:
What's this, what's the holes for, what you doing?
Fidgeting with that ball of string he carries,
untangling a flossy foot of it to tauten,
his eyes slippery, drifting the way they do,
around me without our gaze quite meeting.

I'm planting my rosebushes, I tell him.

He unsettles me, but I'm patient with him:
he means no harm, and it's not his fault.

So, *Why are you?* he asks. And I smile back.
Well, who knows! It's traditional—like those,
see at the ends of the other rows?
Because roses are pretty? But also it's claimed
that they're an alarm plant. Whatever blight
or pest might infest the vines should attack them first.

He looks doubtful; there's no telling
if he's grasped a word I've said. *Especially,*
I say, elaborating anyway,
if like me you don't use pesticides.

What's pesticides? he asks—and suddenly
I hear Oli's voice—when, though?—saying,
Okay, so try pesticides. His tone and his stance
signaling how patient he's being;
that nothing could matter less…

And I remember, yes,
I've just complained about the extra work of the roses—
not really to complain but hoping he'll help.
Oli enjoys the roses. So I'd think,
Maybe this year he'll be less busy,
and we'll plant together—and so now,
Maybe he's come to offer…
But it's only to say he has a job; he'll be gone for week.

Oh, they're chemicals, I tell the neighbor's boy,
with a shrug of earth from my shovel,

a spray, usually, to kill bugs.

He nods. His brow furrows. He's been told not to ask,
but Asperger's, so he asks it. *Did you kill your husband,*
is that why you're always out digging, is it to *bury people?*

Now why, I answer with a snort—raking;
tamping—*would you think such a thing?*

(Because Oli's only gone again;
because it's more quietly than that that a life comes to nothing!
There, I've thought it; however the shame of it cuts,
with its hurt so pure and barely there.
The roses no less lovely; ragged in the wind is all.
I'll toil, and you'll watch, worrying at your ball of string;
none of us meaning harm and it no one's fault.
Then Oli will be back, and we'll fix the knots,
remake the old accommodations.)

My mom says no one's seen him for weeks, he says,
I asked her, I said what if she's killed him, like killed him dead,
he says, and she's buried him in the vineyard, under the vines,
and then when you drink the wine, you taste him?
Mom says Joey don't think such things, but it'd be sooo coool.

Wouldn't it, though, sweetheart! I say back, laughing.
How stupidly little it takes to cheer me up.
But life, you'll learn, is full of disappointments.

He weighs his ball of string
in the right hand then the left,
as if the one is loath to accept the other's evidence.

Yeah, he sighs. *That's the word on the street.*

The Stairwell Watch

In the outside stairwell of the arts camp theater I found
a wristwatch. A girl's watch—with a pink rose on the face—
pressed face down into a tuft of grass. You know, the metal
staircase, round the back, up to a rusted-out third floor door?
The mystery door? No one climbed it, except to pose for pics.
And maybe she'd lost it like that—taking a picture.
But I didn't think so. That stoner kid told us that time,
how kids snuck off after dark, you know, in couples?
To this stairwell, to make out and stuff? So I thought,
maybe she just took the watch off, to make out,
and forgot it after. And then, yeah, so if I found her,
could I look her in the eye, even?
                              It was already almost dark.
I'd been feeling, I guess, homesick? So after chow hall
I took a walk. Anyway, I don't know why, exactly,
but after I brushed the dirt off it, the rose on its face,
its rose gold hands, I mounted the stairs with it, and hid.
And I peeked down through the fretwork—so if that couple
came back, I could see who the girl was, and then leave
it somewhere she'd find it. And yeah, two kids did come.
But they just sat all quiet! And I watched. I mean, only
to make out did I know them, and who the girl might be.
But instead—I mean, I *never* use words like that,
not really—it was wild, he just cursed her out. Like,
on a dime, he got so *mad* at her. And she just *let* him be.
When she was sure he was done, she touched his face.
Kiss me, she said. I couldn't hear always, but I did
hear that. And he said back, *I don't want to kiss you.*
Well, I won't repeat it all. Eventually, though, she cried,
and that's when she lifted her hand to her face, her own face,
this time, and I saw her wristwatch. So yeah, I guess she
wasn't even her. There was barely any light now, but I saw it:
it was a wristwatch. I wanted so badly for them to just leave.
So I could uncross my legs, so I could pee. But instead,
they, like, made up, I guess. I didn't watch. Anyway,
it was too dark. I could hear, though… So yeah,
girls still wear watches, then. I guess girls do
a lot of things, but I was 15, what did I know?
Later, after I had watched till their shadows
vanished all the way into the shadows, I laid
the watch back where I'd found it. I laid my hand
flat to the ground around it. To feel, was it still warm.

The Frame Maker's Daughter

1.
There's something to her quietness of gaze that makes me see her:
  the frame maker's daughter, in her house of walls.
  Who one day found her way back to him:
  to the man who sent her cards, handmade, for Christmas,
  for her birthday, even Halloween; and signed them
  with the flourish that she came to learn meant *father*.
When she was 16 years old, and gaunt as a shadow—her mother
  more than two years dead—she landed in his life like the letter
  he'd always hoped for back; but which came almost too late;
  saying, *love our child while there's still time* but then was lost,
  that someone for no reason but old hurt had striven
  to keep from him; but what did that matter now?
She'd come thump on the mat of his life and stayed—
  for four miraculous years—this tranquil child of theirs;
  until he in his turn fell ill, and knew that he would die.
So what could he do to keep loving her but leave her everything?
This house, with its trunks and trunks of books, its big, bare walls;
  this workshop back of the clump of fruit trees,
  with its tools and its workbench and its store of frames?

And because (even if he was never sure of it) she had come
  to love her father, she loved those books—
  just to leaf through them and look—and although
  she'd never learned and *could* never learn to read them
  (it was how her brain worked—which she knew must be why,
  whatever they claimed later, her parents wrenched apart
  when she was little—because of some simple things
  she couldn't do, and wouldn't ever)—
  she began to fill the frames with pages from them:
  with the pages and the frames she thought most beautiful.

2.
She likes the beginnings of the stories best,
she tells me, one of the small clues she offers me,
settling into this dark house that opens around us,
moving room to room to fill it.

Because, she says, of the way the titles float and make shapes—
their white space holding them above the sway of a horizon line.
And she likes the ends, because of how
the last lines of print crowd the sky of them
like a great breath of ash
about to sift down to an emptiness.

There's a book of poems she's particularly fond of also,
although she's less sure why—
the topographies of its free verse blacks and whites perplex her,
the patterns they settle to perplex her,
she can't fix their landscapes in her mind's slow, steady map…
Still, she's sure something's there;
that there's a sense to be made; she can almost grasp it—
unlike the collection of sonnets, I hear her think with a grimace—
although she doesn't know they are called sonnets—
just sees the print in its fat thronged blocks,
page after page almost identical, like slum architecture.

3.
And then a barge woman and her son move to the village;
    he and the girl make friends, and begin to court.
He loves to read, and walks around her house amazed.
He's particularly struck by the living room, her biggest,
    by the framed pages collected on the walls in scores.
There's almost a whole short story; he tries piecing it together—
    tugging the girl from wall to wall to sing it out to her.

Of the four pages missing, they find two quickly,
    one hung in the kitchen, one going up the stairs, the last page.
It's a story from twenty years ago, but set in the city, so to them
    it's modern: about a family of brothers and a machine that flies.
She had liked it because of the shape of the machine's name,
    written always in italics and a different font, *Treeskimmer,*
    and the still missing pages were the ones without it.

One of them's from the middle and they can make their guess at it;
    but the other they need, because it's the next to last page,
    where for some reason three of the brothers go to the sea—
Where somehow they wind up skimming among the gulls,
    scattering torn paper to the waves, with a ponderous, sad
    awkwardness, as if someone or something has died...

She has never seen the sea; she asks what it's like;
    and he promises to tell her, only let them find that page first...
But it's beautiful, the sea; sometimes when he was a kid
    they'd ride the barge to the river's mouth, and moor there.
And he'd look out at how vast it was and dream of traveling it,
    just to ride the slap of it into the wide, lovely world.
Yes, she says, though she's never felt the least tug of such a dream;
    wants simply to stay right here, in the house by the forest
    that she was born in and has come back to.

4.
Now they are at the door of her bedroom—
just to check, he says, although she knows the page won't be there;
and he has stopped at the door in wonder;
and has gone in slowly, looking.
It's a young woman's room,
the fabrics soft, in colors men call red or purple,
knowing that women have subtler, more careful terms for them,
like salmon, or lilac, or bruised thigh—laughing and exclaiming,
Red? Purple? These are nothing like red or purple!

But what has him staring are the five framed pages,
their frames the most fanciful he's ever seen,
in their colors that he can't believe a man,
her father the frame maker, thought up—with their oddball shapes
and their decorative carved laceries and intaglios.
Inside them sit five free verse poems,
their lines aligned and left-justified as though to anchor them,
their right sides like tidelines.

He bends to read out loud a stanza, from the frame by her pillow,
and then a few words of it again, feeling them shift and
clarify inside him, from a savor towards a sense.
She stands pressed behind him with her chin on the prow
of his back, studying the poem with him over his shoulder.
He touches a finger to its right contours.
This is the shape, he says,
the sea marks the sand with when it breathes.

5.
When for the first time she wakes next to him,
   the room through its closed curtains is delicate with light;
   quite bright enough for her to watch him breathe.
She watches him breathe.
She listens to him breathe.

From the room's five walls the poems
   look down on them like portholes,
   each with its shoreline, as if wherever the two of them
   aim from here, how might they miss land?
Her eyes go from one that could hold anything to the next.

If I could read you, she asks, what would you have to tell me?
Her eyes as she comes to me do not flinch; I see her
   from as close as I see you.
I watch her breathe.
I watch you breathe.

In Memoriam Robert Jarrett Waldron

"O sage, Dichter, was du tust? —Ich rühme.
Aber das Tödliche und Ungetüme,
wie hältst du's aus, wie nimmst du's hin? —Ich rühme."

~Rainer Maria Rilke, "O sage, Dichter…"

My father died this Tuesday… I'm sorry—I see
the words on the page, but not how to mean them…
My father, died, this Tuesday. You in this room
knew him, I suspect, better than I did—I suspect
knowing him less whole, you saw only the truer
part of him. Even before founding this reading
series, this "shared continent" of yours, he was a
poet "of confessions, of the small lyric tale
of who did what to whom, not meaning to, and how
it hurt." You may know those lines; what you may not know,
what he never wrote of, as far as I can tell,
was how he loved his children, my brother Grainge and me,
into a cessation of engagement; as adults,
we withdrew to our three corners of the ring,
rarely to risk the touch of gloves. Before June, I'd
seen the old man once in six years. But then he fell
ill, and sent for us, and I came… And so I can
stand here, and feel, well, some warmth of him in my arms.
Too slim a weight, perhaps—less than a son should feel?
Yes. But it is something. Tomorrow at his church,
as you know, is the official memorial.
This one's the rehearsal. I'm hoping that the grace
you've learned here to bestow on homilies like mine
will buoy me; because tomorrow will be harder;
perhaps, without your help, too hard. I have no church.
Nor, of course, was my father, not as most people
measure it, a man of faith. What he believed in,
he wrote, was "not belief but worship"; his faith was
"not faith but praise." He sang and prayed his heart out with
the Christians, while remaining, or so he claimed, a heathen.
I have my doubts. I suspect worship converted him.

He worshipped broadly. He kept a log for it, of what
to worship next. We two were there, quite often. Even
as kids, we'd know it was our turn: he'd hold us more,
do more with us, shift to study us as we spoke.
Usually, we'd be paired with some other item,

37

like swimming, cycling, something he hoped we'd come
to love together... I'll tell one story. For five weeks
we went caving. I did love it, in fact, and he
loved it, you know what the Bluffs are like—no one who
grows up in Barracks Gap can help knowing, at least
by reputation—the Bluffs caves are spectacular.
And then they're terrifying: always that fear you
might be lost. But I wasn't deterred—which he took
pains to praise. You know: "It's when it's hard to worship
that the worship starts." I was 16—of an age
to wince when somebody in my life went all pet
piety on me. But I did want to cave. I nodded with.
And in secret bought a guidebook, with wonderful
charts, which I studied till I had by heart. And trip
after trip, I grew easier with them—aware
that at any time he might declare the program
had moved on, that *this* trip was our last—so falling
harder, faster, as with a holiday romance.
And at first, both my passion and my flair, the work
he took for flair, delighted him. He let me lead;
and I went where in the caves I had read to go.
There's a poem from then, "The Bluffs"? He inscribed it
to me. It imagines being lost in the pitch dark,
and admits to the wish to *be* lost, and the itch
of dissatisfaction at *not* being...
                                    And then,
of course, we did get lost. I took a wrong turn and
he followed. I took another, and I knew it
must be wrong. Which... Well, I *was* stubborn, and I was
stupid, but the point was, I was also quite young.
Why, I thought, can't he tell: take charge? Instead, there was
a tunnel it seemed we could maybe squeeze through and
I squeezed down it. And he followed. But it narrowed;
he got stuck... His arms were thrust out in front of him,
that was something; so after a while, a long while,
I had his sweatshirt tugged off, and he could squinch free.
But then we were in a cavern. Massive; featureless;
and who knew where. I was slumped with my back to
the wall, knees to my chest; I shook, and shook, the breath
wheezed out of me in bolts. "My kind of cathedral,"
was what my father said. A whisper, but it echoed.
He laid his hand on my shoulder; sat by me;
took out the thermos and the sandwiches. He was,

I could see but not accept, quite deeply happy.
We ate in silence. We sat. He reached for my flashlight—
his was off—and extinguished it. We sat there
in the absolute blackness, hearing each other breathe.
Till my panic dimmed to a kind of resignation,
and his rapture to something sane... Ha! My dad
the psalmodist. And his brave, god-drunk epiphanies.
Forgive me. To be his son, without being a
child, I do find that tough... We got back as we'd come,
him leading now, but not much fuss. Well, I did turn
my ankle, and of course had to lean on him. That
was the end of the caving, and again he'd won.

My task now, if I have it right, is to praise him.
It should be easy. I loved my father, I looked
up to him, my mother died just as I turned ten
and he became our only parent, he raised us
with love and fervor, he was there. But it was dad
who taught me about praise, and what he taught was,
praise without challenge, without color, praise that isn't
hard is thin. Do I believe this, I try not to,
but in his case? Despite myself, I find it true.

He was spectacular; he was terrifying;
he was most comfortably himself measuring
himself against the dark, and the emptiness, to sing
into their resonance of scale; he loved to fail,
to finger the bits of the broken song. He was
delighted by what he couldn't find ways to like—
the wheeze of barrel organs, cell-phones, the smell of beer—
he laughed at what peeved him and he became endearing.
He loathed the hymn "All Things Bright and Beautiful"—
in church warbling the Monty Python variant,
"All things dull and ugly, all creatures short and squat"—
not, he averred, to drown out the original,
only as ballast to it. He taught me to read;
he sang in the car; he smoked. (Rarely! I reacted
as though to *clouds* of smoke!) He overpowered me;
all my life I was so young and small. Nursing him
these last months began, perhaps, as a small revenge.
It became more tender; perhaps wholly tender.
Burying him now I am at a loss.

Derek Kannemeyer's recent books include the novel *The Memory Addicts* (2022), the poetry collections *You Go In By The Gate That Isn't There* (2023) and *Mutt Spirituals* (2021), the light verse collection *A Betabestiary* (2023), and the four act *Play of Gilgamesh* (2019). Kirkus Reviews named his photography/non-fiction study *Unsay Their Names* (2021), about the fall from grace of Richmond's Lost Cause statuary, one of their 100 Best Indie Books of 2021. Its photographs were the featured fall 2021 exhibition at Richmond's Black History Museum, and poems from *Mutt Spirituals* won the inaugural chapbook prize from the Irish journal *Blue Nib*. His website is www.petalridge.com.